AUG 0 7 2023

S0-EYH-853

Middleton Public Library
7425 Hubbard Avenue
Middleton, WI 53562

# Career Planning in the
# GIG ECONOMY

Stuart A. Kallen

San Diego, CA

© 2023 ReferencePoint Press, Inc.
Printed in the United States

**For more information, contact:**
ReferencePoint Press, Inc.
PO Box 27779
San Diego, CA 92198
www.ReferencePointPress.com

ALL RIGHTS RESERVED.
No part of this work covered by the copyright hereon may be reproduced or used in any form or by any means—graphic, electronic, or mechanical, including photocopying, recording, taping, web distribution, or information storage retrieval systems—without the written permission of the publisher.

---

LIBRARY OF CONGRESS CATALOGING-IN-PUBLICATION DATA

---

Names: Kallen, Stuart A., 1955- author.
Title: Career planning in the gig economy / by Stuart A. Kallen.
Description: San Diego, CA : ReferencePoint Press, Inc., 2023. | Includes
   bibliographical references and index.
Identifiers: LCCN 2022037140 (print) | LCCN 2022037141 (ebook) | ISBN
   9781678204761 (library binding) | ISBN 9781678204778 (ebook)
Subjects: LCSH: Vocational guidance--Juvenile literature. | Gig
   economy--Juvenile literature.
Classification: LCC HF5381.2 .K347 2022  (print) | LCC HF5381.2  (ebook) |
   DDC 331.702--dc23
LC record available at https://lccn.loc.gov/2022037140
LC ebook record available at https://lccn.loc.gov/2022037141

# CONTENTS

**Introduction**    **4**
Not a Traditional Job

**Chapter One**    **8**
What Is the Gig Economy?

**Chapter Two**    **20**
Are Gig Jobs Right for You?

**Chapter Three**    **31**
Plunging In

**Chapter Four**    **42**
Making the Gig Economy Work for You

Source Notes    54
For Further Research    57
Index    59
Picture Credits    63
About the Author    64

## INTRODUCTION

# Not a Traditional Job

Today an estimated one-third of workers are employed in what is known as the gig economy. In the gig economy, workers tend to be employed part-time. They might work several contract jobs, or gigs, at once. They can also take or refuse new gigs that might come along. This is distinct from more traditional notions of employment, which typically entail working full-time for a single company, often for many years. These newer job holders are referred to by many titles, including *gig workers*, *freelancers*, *side hustlers*, *on-demand employees*, *consultants*, and *independent contractors*. Although the terms may vary, gig workers are participating in an alternative workforce that is growing faster than the traditional job market. In the gig economy, an average worker might be grocery shopping for others during the day, delivering take-out food at night, and blogging for pay about their gigs on weekends. Robin Chase, cofounder of the car-sharing company Zipcar, puts it this way: "My father had one job in his life, I've had six in mine, my kids will have six at the same time."[1]

When Chase's father began his career in the 1960s, most jobs were clearly defined. Employees were given specific tasks to perform by their employers. A worker could follow a distinct career path to a better job and collect a bigger paycheck. In exchange for showing up every day and satisfactorily doing their jobs, employees usually received paid vacations, medical insurance, and other benefits. Workers expected their employers to help them maintain financial security and achieve success. When Chase's children grow up they might work several jobs at once while looking for other opportunities. They can expect to spend their work lives acquiring new job skills in hopes of moving into more stable positions. Or they will simply persist as on-demand contract workers.

Diane Mulcahy, a business professor who created a master of business administration course on the gig economy at Babson College, says the old rules do not apply in the gig economy. People who seek success in the modern job market need to be proactive about their employment. This means controlling their work situation and pushing for positive outcomes rather than passively waiting for instructions from a boss. Mulcahy calls this confident attitude the "opportunity mindset." As she explains, "Workers with opportunity mindsets see themselves as active creators, builders, and architects of their own career trajectories, not the recipients of them. They accept and expect to generate their own customized version of security, stability, and identity that is separate from any one company or organization. They create their own visions of success and work to achieve it."[2] This puts a lot on the shoulders of the workers, but many newer companies cater to gig workers, finding it easier and cheaper to work with them than with traditional employees.

> "Workers with opportunity mindsets see themselves as active creators, builders, and architects of their own career trajectories."[2]
>
> —Diane Mulcahy, business professor

## Learn It Before You Earn It

You might be among those who want to generate your own version of success in the gig economy. If so, you need to do your research prior to plunging in. Before you sign up for gigs on an app, you need to understand the specific details of the job you seek. Although it can be tedious to read the fine print on an app website, you should understand exactly what kind of work you will be doing, what is expected of you, and when and how you will get paid. And you need to understand your own costs if you are using a personal vehicle or have to purchase equipment such as all-weather clothing for a delivery gig.

Getting paid for a one-time-only project or a series of on-demand tasks can be an unpredictable way to earn money. Profits might be flowing on busy days and nonexistent during slow periods. Because gig work is varied and random, you need to plan ahead and save money to have enough for your budgetary needs every month. This requires you to be organized and informed.

Those who work for a rideshare app such as Uber or a delivery site such as Postmates do not necessarily need to promote themselves. But freelancers who perform project-based jobs ranging from tutoring to website development need to build basic business skills. As economic journalist Deanna Ritchie makes clear, these freelancers might feel independent, but they are still responsible for treating their gigs as a traditional, small business. "If a business is going to be profitable, it cannot be a casual venture,"[3] she maintains. Freelancers need to create a business en-

*Those who work for rideshare apps like Uber can usually adapt to the gig with ease. But freelancers who perform project-based jobs like tutoring need to build more marketing skills to be successful.*

tity with a company name, website, logo, and social media presence. They must also learn to manage a small office, negotiate prices, read and write contracts, keep financial and tax records, and build a gig portfolio. Those who fail to manage their self-employment like a small business might find they are being taken advantage of by the gig companies or the customer base they have built.

## Thinking Differently About Work

Basic business essentials are not difficult to learn. There are hundreds of websites, videos, and courses online that focus on teaching skills such as negotiating, sales, and financial management. With this knowledge, gig workers can chart a path that allows them to decide when to work, for whom to work, and how to best perform their jobs. They can quit their full-time jobs, pursue work they enjoy, start small businesses, and even work remotely while traveling the world. By developing an eye for opportunity and a strategic approach to business, gig workers can create a career that allows them to focus on what they need today and what they hope to achieve in the future.

# CHAPTER ONE

# What Is the Gig Economy?

The word *gig* has long been associated with the jobs freelance musicians take to play live at a venue. To get a gig, a musician might contact several music bookers and bar owners. When musicians land a gig, they engage in negotiations to set a date and time, payment, and other details. Freelance musicians often promote their gigs themselves and provide their own instruments and sound equipment. There is no guarantee of further employment when the gig is over. Someone who practices a lot and works hard might find success in the entertainment industry provided they create music others want to hear. Those who rely on music to earn a living pay their own medical insurance, keep tax records, and try to save enough money to get them through dry spells when gigs are not available.

Until recently, few people could imagine an economy in which millions of people managed their jobs like self-employed musicians. But in today's gig economy, independent workers can be found in almost every type of industry. Like musicians, these workers provide a short-term service and are paid after each gig is finished. With hard work and unique skills, some of these workers can leverage their gigs into successful careers. Yet others might remain stuck with insecure employment, working several gigs and perhaps searching for full-time jobs.

## Uberized Work

Whatever the pros and cons of the gig economy, there is little doubt that it represents a huge change in the labor market. Although many people have worked multiple jobs in the past to make ends meet, the notion of a gig economy took off when the rideshare app Uber went viral during the mid-2010s. The Uber app connects customers to independent workers who drive passengers in their own cars. Uber's algorithm finds rides for customers, determines a driver's pay, and takes a percentage of the money for the company. This business model, sometimes called *uberization*, has been adopted by hundreds of companies that have created apps to connect customers to gig workers who provide services on demand.

*The word* gig *has long been associated with the jobs freelance musicians take to play live at a venue. There is no guarantee of further employment when the gig is over.*

The number of services that have been uberized include cooking, beauty and wellness, package and food delivery, car washing, teaching, tech support, home repair services, and more. App developer Nikhil Bansal sees this development in a positive light. He claims, "Uberization has not only introduced newer ways for buying and selling services, it has also moved the focus of the world economy. . . . If you can make the product or service accessible to the consumer, you can build a successful business."[4] For those like Bansal, the gig economy is about opportunity. However, many gig workers are still working multiple jobs—like those in the past—to pay the bills.

> "If you can make the product or service accessible to the consumer, you can build a successful business."[4]
>
> —Nikhil Bansal, app developer

There are many popular gig apps. TaskRabbit is for those who do home repairs, cleaning, furniture moving, and other basic tasks. Instacart is an on-demand shopping and grocery delivery service. Grubhub connects local restaurants with independent takeout delivery drivers. Freelance employment platforms such as Upwork and Fiverr connect customers to independent workers in almost every imaginable field, including graphic design, writing, video animation, and entertainment. There are hundreds of other gig apps that are less popular than these well-known examples, and some are highly specific. For example, the Grabr app lets users obtain any item from around the world, delivered by travelers who are visiting specific locations.

## From Free Agents to the Financially Strapped

In 2022 around 60 million people identified as freelancers, independent contractors, or gig workers. The McKinsey Global Institute research center divides these workers into four broad categories. Around one-third are categorized as *free agents* who

## Making the Gig Economy Sustainable

Consumers have come to expect their goods and groceries to be delivered as quickly as possible. But delivery companies have a hard time retaining freelance drivers, who jump from one app to another while seeking to maximize their pay. Tom Fiorita, chief executive officer of the delivery company Point Pickup, believes this business model is not sustainable.

Fiorita employs 350,000 freelance drivers who make deliveries for major grocers, including Walmart and Kroger. In 2021 Fiorita wanted to ensure that his business would continue to attract independent flex-work drivers. This led him to launch a benefits app called GigPoint. Drivers using GigPoint accumulate points that can be redeemed for cash bonuses, paid vacations, and discounts on products and services. GigPoint also offers affordable health and dental insurance plans. Fiorita explained why there is a need for services such as GigPoint:

> We've recognized that the gig economy is becoming too fractured to be sustainable in the long term, and access to better care benefits for our workers is more necessary than ever. . . . GigPoint will help our network of more than 350,000 Flex Workers build . . . happier and more fulfilling lives. We are looking toward the future of the gig economy by not accepting the status quo.

Quoted in PR Newswire, "Point Pickup Launches New Era in Gig Economy via GigPoint Platform," October 25, 2021. www.prnewswire.com.

---

earn their primary income from gig work. Workers who achieve success as free agents can build careers based on their unique talents. As business professor Diane Mulcahy points out,

> The Gig Economy is an economy of skills, and skilled workers are the winners who take all. Their talents are in demand, so they can command high wages and have the most opportunity to structure and design their own working lives and craft their own futures. They can . . . create a working life that incorporates flexibility, autonomy, and meaning. Skilled workers have the chance to move from good jobs to great work.[5]

11

A larger group of workers in the gig economy, around 40 percent, are classified as *casual earners* by McKinsey. Casual earners make most of their income from full-time jobs and pick up gigs to make extra money in their spare time. These workers have what are called *side gigs* or *side hustles*. Although driving and delivery are the most common side gigs, some casual earners are discovering ways to make money through their hobbies, training, and creative talents. Those with literary skills are writing blogs or ad copy, editing books and articles, and translating documents. People with technical training are building websites, helping others set up online businesses, and developing apps and games. The artistically inclined are customizing clothes, writing songs, making jewelry, and selling paintings and photographs. Accord-

*Although rideshare and delivery are the most common side gigs, some casual earners are discovering ways to make money through their hobbies, training, and other creative talents.*

ing to the DollarSprout Side Hustle Survey, 42 percent of those with side hustles are optimistic about the future of their gigs.

*Reluctant workers*, who make up 14 percent of the on-demand labor pool, earn their primary income from gigs but would prefer full-time employment. A similar number of workers are classified as *financially strapped*. This group includes minimum wage earners who are forced to take on gigs because their full-time jobs do not pay them enough to take care of their financial needs.

## Winners and Losers

There are bound to be winners and losers in any economy made up of satisfied free agents, unhappy reluctant workers, and millions who fall somewhere in between. The differences are exemplified by two workers who use popular gig apps: TaskRabbit worker William Young and Uber driver Rondu Gantt. Young graduated from New York University in 2020 during the height of the COVID-19 pandemic. Most businesses were shut down, leaving Young unemployed with large bills to pay. He signed up on the workers-for-hire app TaskRabbit and went into business installing wall mounts for large televisions. Young was willing to work long hours to achieve his goals. He was only paid around $15 an hour for his first few jobs, but he received high ratings and good reviews for his work. He soon moved up to $25 an hour, and after a few months he was billing customers up to $50 an hour. By 2021 Young had performed more than fourteen hundred jobs, which included mounting televisions, mirrors, air conditioners, and other heavy items. He was listed on TaskRabbit as a five-star Elite Tasker, the site's highest rating, and earned more than $130,000 on the app that year. Young says, "I'm saving most of my income . . . but I do reinvest into my business in terms of buying quality tools, gear, or anything that improves my efficiency. The next step for me is to invest what I earn into another business."[6]

In San Francisco, rideshare driver Gantt had a different experience in the gig economy. Gantt signed up with Uber in 2018 to

> "My costs are higher, my pay is the same, so I'm losing money. That's a mathematical reality."[7]
>
> —Rondu Gantt, rideshare driver

supplement his teaching income. The job was barely profitable, but Uber paid drivers weekly bonuses to keep them on the road in the Bay Area, where rideshare drivers are in great demand. But Gantt said the situation changed in 2022 when gas prices in California surged to more than six dollars a gallon: "My costs are higher, my pay is the same, so I'm losing money. That's a mathematical reality. . . . I can't work 16 hours every day. I'm gonna burn out. It's physically demanding to be tired, drinking coffee, under-rested, and driving morning and night."[7]

Gantt's and Young's experiences illustrate the disparities that loom large in the gig economy. Young made good money with nothing more than some professional tools and a strong back. And when people were stuck at home during the pandemic, sales of big-screen televisions surged, creating a demand for Young's specialized service.

Although Gantt's services are in demand, Uber requires drivers to shoulder the expenses associated with buying, maintaining, and fueling late-model vehicles. Mulcahy acknowledges the struggles faced by rideshare drivers, but she says Gantt and others would have likely been driving taxis before the rise of the gig economy. "Uber drivers work under similar circumstances that most taxi drivers always have: they are contractors with no benefits, no overtime or minimum wage, and no access to unemployment insurance," she explains. "But there are many more people willing to be Uber drivers than taxi drivers, in part because they can control when and how much they work."[8]

## Managing Gig Workers with Artificial Intelligence

Supporters of the gig economy like Mulcahy often say that it provides work to those who want to be their own bosses while breaking loose from the restrictions of a traditional nine-to-five job. But

## Good and Bad Feelings About Gigs

Anyone researching the gig economy can find countless articles that list the positive and negative aspects of various gigs. In 2021 the Pew Research Center went beyond the headlines to conduct a survey to determine how gig workers felt about their jobs. According to Pew, around half of workers feel somewhat positive about their gigs, and 25 percent feel very positive.

The reasons people take on gigs can be divided into three roughly equal categories, according to Pew. One-third say they like being their own boss, another third say they take on gigs for fun or to earn money in their spare time. The final third say they work gigs because they have no other job opportunities.

Some who use gig apps are unhappy with their working conditions, the survey found. Thirty percent say they have been treated rudely by customers, 33 percent say they have felt unsafe on occasion while performing their gigs, and 22 percent of all women say they have experienced unwanted sexual advances while gigging. And as the COVID-19 virus remains a constant factor in society, around half of gig workers say they fear being exposed to the virus.

rather than answering to bosses, gig workers are often invisibly supervised by sophisticated artificial intelligence programs that follow their every move.

As with much of the gig economy, Uber has led the way. And the Uber model has provided a template for many other popular apps. Uber algorithms manipulate fares customers pay to bring in the largest percentage of profits. The amount Uber pays drivers for each ride fluctuates constantly; the app raises and lowers fares depending on how many people need rides, how many drivers are available, and other conditions, such as the time of day and the weather. Drivers are unaware of these changes and are required to accept any ride without knowing where the customers are being picked up and where they are going. When there is a surge in demand, drivers receive push notifications and constant pings for the next ride, even before any current ride is completed. If they decide to log off during a busy period, the app begins to look like a video game. It might

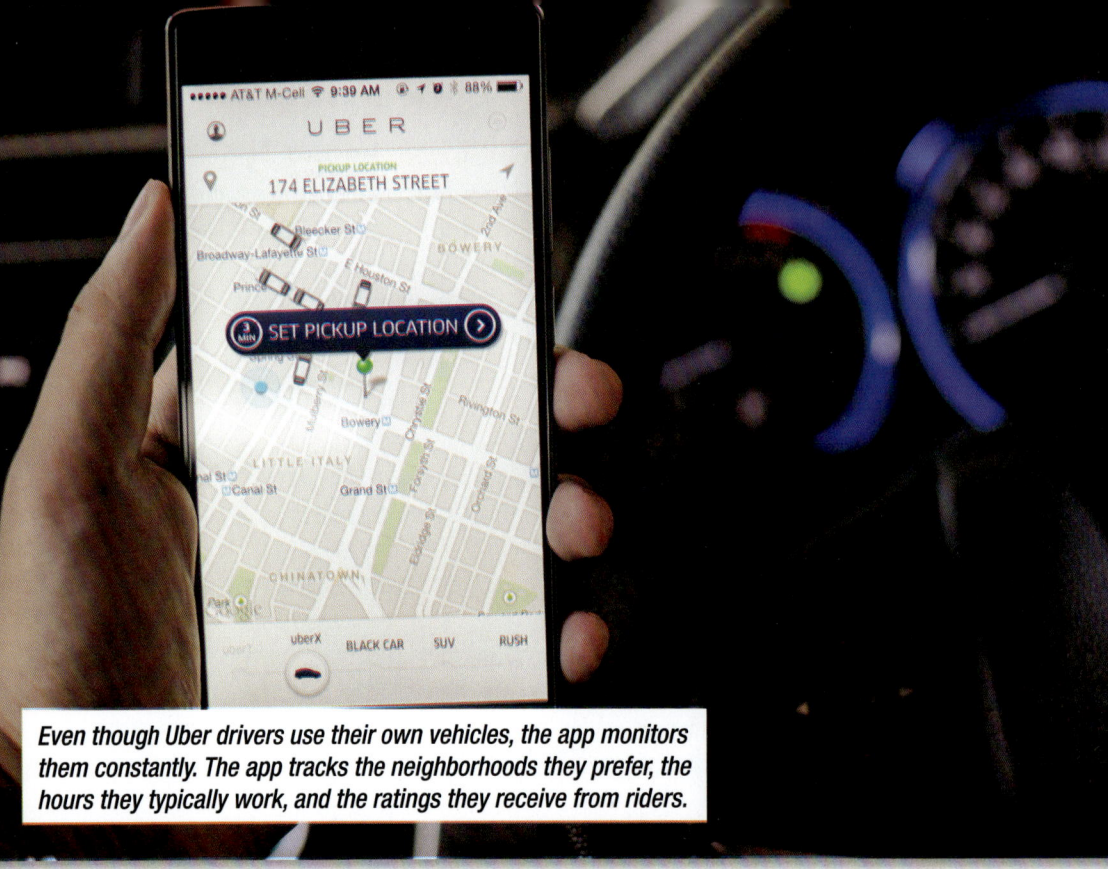

Even though Uber drivers use their own vehicles, the app monitors them constantly. The app tracks the neighborhoods they prefer, the hours they typically work, and the ratings they receive from riders.

unlock a benefit, such as showing how much the next trip is worth. The app might offer a bonus of up to thirty dollars for completing ten more rides. With the rules constantly changing, drivers are unable to determine how much money each ride will bring in. Although Uber increased bonuses as gas prices rose in 2022, the company shortened the length of time drivers have to decide whether to accept a ride from twenty seconds to five seconds. Uber driver Surgeet Singh explains, "Even with all the data we can see and track, it's hard to know what's going on inside the algorithm."[9]

Even though Uber drivers use their own vehicles, the app monitors them constantly. The app tracks how many people they pick up, the neighborhoods they prefer, the hours they typically work, and the ratings they receive from riders. This system allows drivers to accumulate points by working certain hours and maintaining high customer ratings. Points can be redeemed for fuel and car repairs, but they can be very hard to amass because they expire after three months. Taken together, all these measures make it difficult for drivers to pick rides that are profitable and ignore those that are not. Las Vegas driver Anthony Arnold says that these measures contradict claims made about gig work. "They call us independent workers, as if we have control over what goes on in the app," he remarks. "Sure, you can make a bit of money, but it's not going to be on your terms."[10]

## The Economics of the Gig Economy

Less than half of gig workers even understand how their pay is calculated, according to a 2021 survey by the Pew Research Center. This uncertainty has spawned its own gig economy populated by specialists who charge drivers to explain how the rideshare apps affect their profits. According to journalists Jackie Davalos and Drake Bennett, "The difficulty of keeping abreast of these changes is feeding a niche industry of bloggers, YouTubers, consultants, and even venture-capital-backed apps—a kind of gig economy economy."[11]

Harry Campbell launched his career in the gig economy with the *Rideshare Guy* blog. Campbell was an engineer who took on a side hustle as a driver for Uber and Lyft in 2014. When he tried to find out more information about the apps he used and the way he was paid, he found that no one was providing that information. Campbell quit his engineering job to launch his blog, which grew into a comprehensive media operation that includes newsletters, podcasts, and videos aimed at workers trying to boost their income in the gig economy. On YouTube, Torsten Kunert, known as "the Rideshare Professor," teaches courses on maximizing rideshare profits. A company called Solo even has an app for that: launched by a former Uber executive, the app helps drivers figure out how much they will earn for every hour they work.

## No Profits for Platforms

The irony of the gig economy is that while workers are struggling to boost their earnings, most gig platforms themselves are not making money. Uber again exemplifies the problem; although the company brought in $53 billion between 2018 and 2022, it spent about $73 billion expanding its network worldwide and building offices and other infrastructure. Another gig economy giant, DoorDash, charges both restaurants and diners for the service it provides but still lost half a billion dollars in 2021. According to stock analyst Kartik Menon this lack of profits is harming workers:

> [A] glaring similarity of many of these companies is that they continue to rack up staggering losses while barely investing in the equipment or labor of their underlying services. Delivery fees eat into already thin restaurant [profits] and cause chaos for food workers. Uber and its gig-economy brethren hire their frontline workers on a contract basis, meaning they have few obligations to their drivers and delivery people: no health insurance, retirement-savings plans, or consistent pay.[12]

The staggering losses are also hurting the tech economy. Investors have pumped billions into dozens of apps that never caught on. Although most people have heard of Instacart, lesser-known grocery delivery services such as Gorilla, Getir, Jokr, and Buyk all declared bankruptcy in 2022. There are so many of these money-losing gig platforms that Goldman Sachs created a stock index called "Unprofitable Tech" to keep track of them.

Menon is unsure where these trends in the gig economy might be leading. Although major platforms struggle for profitability, there is little doubt that the public has come to depend on many gig services. In 2022 around 24 percent of Americans used a rideshare app at least once a month, and more than 40 percent

> "Uber and its gig-economy brethren ... have few obligations to their drivers and delivery people: no health insurance, retirement-savings plans, or consistent pay."[12]
>
> —Kartik Menon, stock analyst

used a food delivery app, according to Statista. These consumers added hundreds of billions of dollars to the gig economy. And drivers and other on-demand laborers were able to take advantage of this growing demand by pushing for better wages and more transparency in the way they are paid.

The performance of any economic sector can be hard to predict, and the gig economy is no different. This is especially true because the massive growth of gig platforms and freelance workers who use them is a new phenomenon. The 2020 pandemic changed the way consumers shopped for goods and services, and many do not wish to return to the old ways. At the same time, people might be unwilling to pay higher rates for these on-demand services that were once seen as cheap and convenient. Anyone planning a career in this marketplace will need to be informed about and adaptable to the ever-changing landscape of the gig economy.

# CHAPTER TWO

# Are Gig Jobs Right for You?

In the United States, people often talk about achieving the American Dream. For decades, aspiring to reach the American Dream meant finding a good, steady job; buying a home; getting paid vacation time; and seeing a growth in wages over time. Some refer to this as the *forty/forty plan*: work forty hours a week for forty years and retire with enough money to be financially secure. Many people continue to aim for the forty/forty plan. But the goal of settling into a secure forty-year work situation is at odds with the reality of the gig economy.

Most gig jobs are temporary. Earnings may go up, but they can also go down for reasons beyond a worker's control. For this reason, gig workers might have a difficult time obtaining the foundation for the American Dream: buying a home. Banks are reluctant to give mortgages to people whose employment situation varies from month to month. This means gig jobs might not be best suited for someone seeking the traditional American Dream. However, an increasing number of people are pursuing what might be called the new American Dream. They work gigs so they can create their own definition of success. They do not want to surrender their time and energy to the whims of supervisors and bosses forty hours and more each week. They want to live up to their full potential while having enough free time to enjoy life. These beliefs are extremely popular among millennials (born between 1981 and 1996) and

Gen Z (born between 1997 and 2012) workers. According to a 2022 survey by the employment website Randstad, half of all millennials and Gen Zers would rather be unemployed than stuck in a job they did not like. And around 55 percent would quit a job if it interfered with their personal lives or if the company they worked for did not align with their political or social views.

## Sacrificing Comfort for Gigs

Kyle Nossaman is among those seeking the new American Dream. In 2018 Nossaman quit his full-time job as an editor for the outdoors magazine *Gear Junkie*. His dream was to explore America with his wife while living in an old school bus they had turned into a recreational vehicle. Nossaman's new career as a freelance travel writer and editor was meant to pay his expenses.

*An increasing number of people are pursuing what might be called the new American Dream. They want enough free time to enjoy life and will not surrender their time and energy to the whims of supervisors for over forty hours weekly.*

> "We've pared down our possessions (from clothes to shoes, cookware, electronics, etc.) and have learned to live more simply. We . . . buy fewer things, and spend less on entertainment."[13]
>
> —Kyle Nossaman, freelance travel writer

The Nossamans sacrificed the comfort of their luxury apartment to travel the country in the confined quarters of their bus. But they were able to thrive by changing their habits: "We've pared down our possessions (from clothes to shoes, cookware, electronics, etc.) and have learned to live more simply. We shower less, use less electricity (and what we do use is solar-powered), watch less TV, conserve more water, re-wear clothes, cook more, buy fewer things, and spend less on entertainment."[13]

The gig economy caters to such individualized pursuits. And the Nossamans are not alone. The high costs of housing and homeownership are making mobile life more attractive for some seeking the new American Dream. The 2022 spike in gas prices made some reconsider their choices; school buses like Nossaman's get around 8 miles per gallon (3 km/L). But as twenty-eight-year-old freelance tech worker and recreational vehicle owner Jupiter Estrada says, "I'm in a really good position where gas is, essentially, my rent. My backyard is anywhere I want."[14]

Nossaman and Estrada carefully weighed the positive and negative aspects of freelancing before taking up careers in the gig economy. They were willing to forgo steady paychecks and employee benefits such as medical insurance, retirement benefits, and paid vacations. Not everyone is willing to do so. Employment researcher Steve King explains that "some people are cut out for the uncertainty associated with independent work and some are not."[15] Those who approach job uncertainty with self-motivation and ambition can enjoy the freedom and flexibility the gig economy offers.

### Crafting a Career

Sut I. Wong, director of the *BI Business Review*, says prospective gig workers can best deal with job insecurity by clearly defining their employment strengths and passions. Wong calls this

## To Gig or Not to Gig

Despite the gig economy's unique challenges, there are good reasons why people strike out on their own as independent workers. According to author John W. Coleman, the main reason why people prefer gig work is because their full-time jobs are not providing feelings of personal growth. People who repeat the same tasks over and over often feel stagnant at work. They develop difficulties when it comes to paying attention to their repetitive work.

Sometimes a job creates feelings of fear or dread. People who are overworked often experience burnout and might have feelings of anxiety. They often lose sleep, feel exhausted, and develop bad dietary habits. Coleman advises, "If you regularly feel dread at approaching your work, it's time to seriously consider changing it or leaving it behind. Your life is short and precious, and your work should enrich it."

People also quit their jobs when the workplace becomes toxic. No one should have to experience bosses and coworkers who yell, insult others, or act unethically. As Coleman writes, "Some workplaces are consistently harmful to your physical or emotional health. If you find yourself in that unenviable position, it's time to move on."

John W. Coleman, "6 Signs It's Time to Leave Your Job," *Harvard Business Review*, February 8, 2022. https://hbr.org.

---

process "job crafting." She explains that "by proactively examining what kinds of work they find most meaningful or interesting, actively seeking out opportunities that match those preferences, and developing the skills necessary to succeed in those areas, workers can leverage the freedom and autonomy that gig work offers to craft a job that works best for them."[16]

The best way to practice job crafting is to make three columns on a sheet of paper labeled *motives*, *strengths*, and *passions*. Under *motives* write down what motivates you to seek a career in the gig economy. It might be money in the short term. Or your motivation might consist of a long-term objective such as starting your own company or independently achieving success in a specific field. The *strengths* column should contain a list of the abilities and talents that you can apply toward achieving your goals.

The *passions* column should highlight what you would love most in your work life. It might include anything from art and music to traveling and teaching.

Although writing down your goals is a great way to assess your wants and needs, it is important to be realistic during the job-crafting process. You might be motivated to become a fashion designer or game developer, but competition is fierce in these fields. If you are sufficiently motivated and passionate about your career, you can apply your strengths toward achieving these difficult-to-attain goals. In the meantime, keep your dream front and center while working a variety of gigs in related areas. For example, a prospective game developer can pay the bills with gigs in web design, animation, coding, or app development while learning on the job and acquiring skills that will be helpful in the future.

Another important part of job crafting requires a careful assessment of how much money you need and what your skills are worth. Experts recommend that gig workers set a minimum-income target. This is the smallest amount of money you would be happy

*If you are spending forty hours or more per week to attain your minimum-income goal, you might be better off working at a full-time job that provides health insurance and other benefits.*

with; studies show that independent workers who make $30,000 annually doing what they love can be just as happy as those who make two or even five times that amount. Setting an income target allows you to measure how successful you are in achieving your goals. You can reassess your situation and make changes if you are falling short of your minimum-income target.

Setting a minimum-income target should be linked to how many hours you are willing to work each week. If you are spending forty hours or more to attain your minimum-income goal, you might be better off working at a full-time job that provides health insurance and other benefits. But if you love what you are doing and are committed to success, then the time you dedicate to your gig might not matter.

## Committing to Your Goals

Job crafting can be a lonely pursuit in the gig economy. As Wong writes, "Part of what makes it more difficult . . . is the lack of built-in support structures, resources, and role models to help workers job craft on their own. . . . In the gig economy, workers have to proactively find (or build) their own communities to help them job craft."[17] Communities can be found on gig employment websites—such as Fiverr and Upwork—that run forums in which workers can connect with others seeking advice. Other sites are run by gig workers who are focused on their specific fields. For example, the Gig Workers Collective brings together a community of grocery shoppers and rideshare drivers.

> "In the gig economy, workers have to proactively find (or build) their own communities to help them job craft."[17]
>
> —Sut I. Wong, director of the BI Business Review

Another part of job crafting concerns sharing your gig goals with friends and family members. People who discuss their ambitions with others are more likely to hold themselves accountable, which leads to success. A 2019 study by the Association for Talent Development proved this point. Researchers found that people who set out alone to complete a goal had only a 10 to 25 percent chance of success. Those who promised a friend or loved one that they would achieve a specific goal increased their success rate to 65 percent. The greatest success rate was seen among those who chose an accountability partner—someone to hold them to their promises. The subjects in the study who met with an accountability partner on a regular basis to discuss their setbacks and achievements saw an astounding 95 percent success rate. The same success was seen in those who joined an accountability group made up of people who had similar goals. Journalist Thomas Oppong explains: "If you want to take accountability to a whole new level, especially on [a] regular basis, consider joining a habit group where members keep track of their results. If you are serious about achieving your goals, it can be one of your most potent sources of support and accountability. . . . If you want to improve your chances of success, use the power of accountability."[18]

## Finding a Balance

Author and dance teacher Allison Nichol Longtin never had a problem holding herself accountable. Longtin had committed herself to a career in dance by the time she was in high school. But she knew it would be difficult to realize her dreams in the highly competitive world of dancing. This led her to use her job crafting skills to turn her passion for dancing into a moneymaking gig. Longtin worked a series of low-paying jobs, including nanny and retail sales assistant, while remaining committed to her dream: "I did this kind of work for years."[19] Eventually, Longtin made a commitment to pursue her dream as a choreographer and dance teacher. She was able to land some gigs, but found herself working up to sixty hours a week without making much money. This led Longtin to abandon the

> "If you want to improve your chances of success, use the power of accountability."[18]
>
> —Thomas Oppong, journalist

## Holding Yourself Accountable

Stephen Newland is a financial counselor who works with groups of people who have failed to achieve their monetary goals. Newland always asks his participants why they failed to take steps to improve their situation. He says he hears the same answer again and again: "I didn't have anyone to hold me accountable." Newland teaches them various methods to become accountable. One tool he recommends is signing a contract addressed to yourself that outlines your commitment. There is an app for that, called stickK, which provides a commitment contract form. The form is referred to as a binding agreement with yourself. Users pick a goal, describe the steps they are willing to take to achieve it, and set a timeline. The app requires users to write regular progress reports. If users fail to hold themselves accountable, the app notifies friends and family who have volunteered to participate in the program.

Although helpful, an app is not necessary for those who wish to hold themselves accountable while seeking a career in the gig economy. It is simply a tool that utilizes the psychological power of accountability to help users achieve their goals.

Stephen Newland, "The Power of Accountability," Association for Financial Counseling & Planning Education, 2018. www.afcpe.org.

---

gig economy in favor of a full-time job in the nonprofit arts sector. She continued to teach dance as a side hustle. Longtin says that this move allowed her to find "the sweet spot and get the best of both worlds: stable income [in the nonprofit sector] earned doing a job that connected me to a sense of purpose and service, and that aligned with my core values, and creative work in dance that connected me to my deepest sense of self."[20]

After attaining the sweet spot, Longtin did not rest. She developed her writing skills and started working as a freelance writer and school curriculum developer. In 2022 her success in these gig pursuits allowed her to resign from her full-time job. Dance lessons provide about 40 percent of Longtin's income, and the writing gig makes up the rest. Longtin provides perspective on her career arc: "The lessons I learned from my early career in dance, where I worked [low-paying jobs] to support myself, prepared me for my now fully-freelance career as a writer and dance teacher by showing me what didn't work for me."[21]

Not everyone is willing to trade the security of full-time work for a fully freelance career. But many who do so find a stronger sense of well-being when they depend solely on themselves for their income. In 2021 a survey of over six thousand freelance workers by the MBO Partners business group showed that two-thirds agreed with the statement "I feel more secure working independently."[22] These independent workers believe that having more than one source of income is better than depending on a single employer. Like Longtin, they can change or augment gig jobs when economic conditions require them to do so. And many are glad to be free of the boredom and burnout sometimes associated with traditional full-time jobs.

The independence associated with gig work can lead to personal fulfillment. According to King, "If someone chooses to be independent they are much more likely to be satisfied than someone who was forced into it. . . . People who chose to be independent are much more likely to have prepared for independence . . . and are more likely to . . . hit their income targets."[23]

## Not Always Working

Whereas Longtin finds happiness pursuing her artistic career goals, David Aria finds himself stressed out about his gig. Aria is a freelance audio engineer; he works in recording studios where he operates sound equipment and produces music tracks. Aria is also a musician who performs live on occasion, but he says none of his gigs are paying enough for him to get ahead. "I would love to be financially stable. I don't particularly like the idea of freelancing as a sort of permanent solution," he states. "I'm a musician as well, I have my own goals, but I've had to put them aside. It's like, I'm good at saving money, I'm not that great at making it yet."[24]

Aria is not alone; many people find it difficult to earn a living in the gig economy. This is especially true for those who have skills

*Many people find it difficult to earn a living in the gig economy. This is especially true for those who have skills in fields in which the supply of workers outpaces the demand for their services, such as audio engineering.*

in fields in which the supply of workers outpaces the demand for their services. In Aria's case, the freelance website Fiverr has hundreds of listings for people willing to mix and master song tracks. Some offer basic services for as little as five dollars per song.

Aria might have a better chance at achieving the new American Dream if he sets a goal of finding full-time work in a music store or an established recording studio. He could make a commitment to his goal of becoming a freelance audio engineer while making an accountability commitment to himself or someone in his community. Aria could gain experience working side hustles such as teaching music, writing jingles for advertisements, or playing as a session musician on recordings made by others.

### Assess Your Needs

The stories of Longtin and Aria and show that there are positive and negative aspects to seeking careers in the gig economy. Those who succeed, such as Longtin, can juggle multiple unrelated gigs while remaining accountable to their career commitments. They are willing to take risks, look for new and better ways to get things done, and enjoy new challenges.

If the new American Dream looks good to you, assess your wants and needs before you jump in. Ask yourself what you want from gig jobs. Are you seeking temporary work to earn extra money during a break from school or between full-time jobs? Or do you see gig jobs as a stepping-stone to something bigger, such as acquiring skills and contacts to become a successful entrepreneur? Perhaps you want to turn a hobby into a profession or pursue a career in the arts while working gig jobs to make ends meet. Gig jobs are flexible enough to meet many of these needs. It is up to you to decide what you want and whether gig jobs can play a part in your career plans.

## CHAPTER THREE

# Plunging In

Before the rise of the gig economy, job options for young people were limited. Students hoping to grow their college funds or pay family expenses were often limited to working in fast food restaurants, retail shops, and grocery stores. These minimum wage jobs did not offer much flexibility or opportunity for growth. With the evolution of the gig economy, these limitations have disappeared. Almost anyone can find gigs whatever their age. High school students can find simple gigs, such as dog walking, or they can jump into careers in fashion, gaming, tech, and the arts.

Almost all gig platforms, including Instacart and TaskRabbit, require users to be at least eighteen years old. But gig apps are only one option among many for those seeking freelance work. Younger workers can promote their skills through social media, personal websites, networking, and word of mouth. Self-promotion requires extra effort, but those who take the initiative learn valuable skills that can be used to build careers over time.

If you have a way with words, blogging is a great way to plunge into the gig economy. The internet is full of blogs by kids as young as seven who write about their hobbies, outdoor activities, favorite television shows, beloved books, and other topics. Some of the best blogs are published by *National Geographic Kids*, *Sports Illustrated for Kids*, and other national publications.

Blogging has many advantages. You can work from home, or anywhere in the world, while earning a little extra money.

*Before the rise of the gig economy, job options for young people were limited. Now high school students can more easily find simple gig jobs such as dog walking.*

You can share your personal opinions, ideas, life hacks, and almost any other info in a blog. Blogging can be fun if you love to write, and the experience you gain can one day lead to work as a journalist, novelist, advertising copywriter, screenwriter, or related career.

## Find a Niche

Setting yourself apart from the crowd, or finding your niche, is the key to success in the gig economy. This is especially true for blogging. Although you might think your experiences are limited, almost everyone has a unique perspective to offer. Do you have a great memory for sports statistics? Do you know everything there is to know about your favorite band or movie star? Are you a camper or backpacker?

Vicky Chen, an avid reader and writer, began her blogging career while she was a high school student in 2017. Chen was obsessed with young adult fiction and filled her blog, *Vicky Who Reads*, with reviews of her favorite books, interviews with writers, and advice for other teen bloggers. After launching her blog, Chen expanded her reach, becoming what is known as a *bookstagrammer*. This Instagram niche is inhabited by book lovers who post arty pictures of their favorite books. Her reading-related photos helped drive traffic to her blog site. In 2020 Chen explained her journey into the world of blogging:

> "I've become a better, more empathetic and caring person because of [my book-blogging gig], and I could not be more grateful for that."[25]
>
> —Vicky Chen, blogger

> I've certainly loved keeping *Vicky Who Reads* up for over two years, and it's been such a lifeline where I've been able to make so many genuine connections with wonderful people. It's been an ever-present friend when I'm feeling lonely or trapped, and has been there through one of the most formative times of my life. I've become a better, more empathetic and caring person because of it, and I could not be more grateful for that.[25]

In 2021, when Chen started college, she decided to change the name of her blog to *Vicky Again*. In addition to her new blog on the popular blogging website WordPress, Chen writes for the *Barnes & Noble Teen Blog*, the *Shelf Awareness* newsletter, and *Strange Horizons* magazine.

## Promote Yourself

If you want to earn money from a blog or any other type of gig, there are steps you can take to promote yourself. Think of your gig as a product you want to sell, then create a memorable brand for yourself that will resonate with the public. Branding involves producing graphic emblems called logos, memorable catchphrases, and short taglines. All are meant to work together to create a memorable public image for your gig.

Once you establish a brand, it can be used to create a website. WordPress offers a free, user-friendly website builder that is extremely popular; around half of all websites on the internet run on the WordPress platform. Use your search engine to find information about building a website, picking a web-hosting service, and ways to keep your website secure from hackers. WordPress offers free and premium themes, which offer different features. Theme subjects include website templates for blogs, e-commerce, education, and photography. Test each theme to see what best suits your gig. The site offers checkboxes that allow you to add menu items such as your biography and contact information.

*It is a good idea to promote your brand using a website. WordPress offers a free, user-friendly website builder platform that runs about half of all websites on the internet.*

Personalize your website by writing copy that includes the types of gigs you have to offer, why a customer would benefit by hiring you, and what you charge for various services. Once your gig is under way, you can add positive customer reviews. Update your website often with photos, memorable quotes, short tutorials, behind-the-scenes videos, and other clickable content.

Your website will act as a foundation for your social media strategy. This involves spreading the word about your gig through tweets, emails, and posts on Facebook, Instagram, and elsewhere. Use hashtags that identify your gig, such as *#YAblogger*, *#dogwalker*, or *#makinglivemusic*. Once these steps are completed, you can promote your gig to friends and family members and ask them to do the same. Tap into your target audience by joining online communities where your product will be well received.

### Do What You Love

Promoting a gig on social media takes time, but the effort can pay off. Justin Ellen learned that lesson in 2020 when he was seventeen and running a side hustle as a custom cake baker in New Jersey. Ellen learned to bake from his mother and grandmother when he was only seven. He quickly fell in love with the idea of creating beautiful baked goods. By the time Ellen was fourteen, he was spending hours watching cake tutorial videos on YouTube. Although school kept him very busy, he was determined to launch his baking gig.

Ellen understands that a good social media presence is important for any business, but he did not take it seriously at first. When he was in a hurry, he often posted blurry pictures of his artistic cakes, which sold for as much as $150. Ellen's photos improved, but he noticed that people who posted video content were getting the most hits on Instagram. This led Ellen to make himself the subject of his social media posts. Although he was shy at first, his videos were much more popular than the photos. While baking cakes, Ellen offered advice, gave behind-the-scenes insights into

> "People want to know the person behind the brand and if they enjoy you, they're gonna want to spend money with you."[26]
>
> —Justin Ellen, custom cake baker

his baking processes, and talked about his mentors and inspirations. These videos, delivered with sincerity, helped him quickly gain fifty thousand followers on Instagram. According to Ellen, such videos make "you more relatable. People want to know the person behind the brand and if they enjoy you, they're gonna want to spend money with you."[26]

Before long, Ellen was balancing his life as a high school senior with the demands of his baking gig, which was bringing in $5,000 to $9,000 a month. Ellen said his success changed the way he viewed his gig: "[I'm an] entrepreneur first, then a baker. If you want to be a baker, then go work for someone else."[27] As an entrepreneur, Ellen reinvested his profits back into his business. Rather than purchasing expensive sneakers or other luxury items, Ellen created a line of custom cake mixes and baking tools, which he now promotes on social media. He also offers video classes for aspiring bakers. Ellen's most difficult decision was choosing between his gig and going to college. He decided to forgo school. By 2022, he felt he had made the right decision; Ellen had more than seventy-three thousand Instagram followers and was earning more than $100,000 annually.

### Keep Good Records

Ellen might have been in high school when his cake gig took off, but he took on an important responsibility that had nothing to do with flour and frosting. Ellen was required to report his income to the Internal Revenue Service (IRS) and pay federal and state taxes. And he probably needed to hire a tax accountant to help him fill out the complex forms that self-employed people must file by April 15 every year.

Gig workers must keep more exacting tax records than most full-time workers. Employers withhold, or deduct, taxes from the paychecks they give their employees. When workers file their tax-

## Shipping and Handling

Self-employed workers often take on unexpected roles when they launch their gigs. Those who set out to sell products online often overlook the reality of keeping up with shipping and handling. They need to put their goods in boxes, determine shipping costs, and transport the parcels to the local post office or shipping store. Justin Ellen learned this when he launched his custom cake baking gig. One of his first major hassles was figuring out how to ship his cakes all over the country. With his business still in its infancy, Ellen had to borrow $500 from his parents to buy packing materials and custom-made boxes that featured his logo. Packing his delicate cakes into boxes and getting them to customers was nearly as time-consuming as baking them. Luckily, Ellen had help: "My mum works for me now. She helps me a lot with the backend stuff . . . like deliveries [and shipping]." Those who sell items online and do not have their mum to assist them need to handle the shipping processes on their own or find someone to help do the work.

Quoted in Goh Chiew Tong, "Is It Cake? This 19-Year-Old Netflix Show Contestant Is Making 6 Figures in His Bakery Business," CNBC, May 16, 2022. www.cnbc.com.

---

es, they might get a refund or owe more, but most of their tax bill is already paid. Gig workers do not have anyone withholding their taxes. They are 100 percent responsible for meeting tax deadlines and paying the total amount that is owed. Those who fail to file their forms or pay what they owe in a timely fashion face fines and possible criminal penalties.

Depending on where they live, gig workers might also be required to pay state and city taxes, which vary from place to place. And many municipalities require workers to adhere to health and safety regulations. Those who work in food, child care, hair styling, and other services are often required to obtain occupational licenses. Some states and municipalities require chefs, bakers, and others who work with food to obtain a food handler license. This requirement is meant to stop the spread of foodborne illnesses and disease. Municipalities often have additional obligations aimed at independent workers. For example, the self-employed in San Diego are required to purchase a business license annually for thirty-five dollars, even if they only work on a computer in their home office. Information regarding local taxes and regulations can be found at government websites or at the local chamber of commerce office.

### Have a Business Plan

There are many demands made on gig workers besides paying taxes and following regulations. If you plan on launching your own gig, you might want to draw up a business plan to help you clearly outline the steps you need to take to achieve success. The plan does not need to be long and complicated, but you should take your time when writing it. This will allow you to mull over many aspects of your endeavor that you might otherwise overlook. Brett Helling, the founder of Gigworker.com, insists, "If you run an independent outfit you should still put your plans on paper. Even if no one else but you reads it. The practice of writing a simple business plan forces you to solidify your idea and consider every aspect of the company. . . . [A] good business plan outlines your overall direction, focuses your efforts, and defines the best strategies for you to reach your business goals."[28]

> "[A] good business plan outlines your overall direction, focuses your efforts, and defines the best strategies for you to reach your business goals."[28]
>
> —Brett Helling, founder of Gigworker.com

A basic business plan answers questions that reporters refer to as the five *w*'s: who, what, why, where, and when. Simply put, who are your customers, what are their wants and needs, and why would they give you money for your services? Then you need to answer where you will base your business. Will you be operating out of your bedroom, garage, rented studio, your car, or somewhere else? Finally, when will you have time to run the business? Will you be working on weekends, after class, part-time, or full-time? Answering the five *w*'s up front will provide you with a blueprint for your gig. While it will probably change with time and experience, it might save you from unpleasant surprises later.

## Planning for Income Taxes

As of 2022, the IRS requires independent workers who earn over $400 to pay a 15 percent self-employment tax that is applied to Social Security and Medicare taxes. Tax experts recommend that gig workers set aside about one-third of their earnings in a savings account to pay taxes. Sandra Nam Cioffi, a freelance landscape architect, explains how she deals with taxes: "I have a system where every time I get paid, I immediately roll over a percentage into a separate account, and I don't touch it until tax season."

Freelancers can lower their tax bills by deducting business-related expenses from their total earnings. Deductions can include costs related to use of a personal vehicle, advertising, and maintaining a home office. As a landscape architect, Cioffi can deduct costs that include the landscape design software programs and even the shovel and work clothes she uses. However, the IRS requires proof of expenses; self-employed workers need to save business receipts. Anyone taking business deductions should hire a tax accountant to ensure they are following the complex laws that govern such expenses.

Quoted in Vox, "How to Make the Gig Economy Work for You," December 6, 2019. www.vox.com.

When medical student Olivia Hillier sold a cheap secondhand T-shirt through the resale app Poshmark in 2020, she did not have any long-range plans. But during the 2020 COVID-19 pandemic lockdown, she noticed people were making money selling trendy used clothes on Poshmark. This led her to do some research, draw up a business plan, and launch a side hustle that brought in more than $85,000 in 2021.

When putting together her business plan, Hillier learned who was using Poshmark; the site was popular with young professional women between the ages of twenty-five and forty. What did they want to buy? Vintage pieces. Why did they favor these items? This type of clothing made a bold fashion statement. Hillier also needed to consider when and where she would base her business. Her first commitment was getting her medical degree. She drew up a schedule that would allow her to work while balancing the demands of school. She had an extra room in her home where she could store her clothes, take photos, and fill orders.

When Hillier finishes class on Fridays, she hits the local thrift shops to pick up inventory. On Saturday she sorts and cleans clothes. Sundays are given over to Hillier modeling the outfits and taking pictures. She emphasizes that "good lighting can mean the difference between a $5 and $100 sale."[29] In between classes on Monday, Hillier uploads the photos to her site on Poshmark. When she has time during the week, she packs up the clothes and drops them off at her local post office.

By 2022 Hillier was spending twenty to forty hours a week on her gig, and she was earning more than $5,000 a month. She had one expense she did not initially consider: Poshmark takes 20 percent of every purchase. That led Hillier to branch out. She began selling her clothes on Facebook Marketplace, which does not charge a commission. She likes Poshmark, however, because it provides customer-paid shipping labels with each purchase. This saves her time during the shipping process.

> "You've got to be regimented and have a routine. If I didn't love [selling clothes online] so much, I wouldn't make the time for it."[30]
>
> —Olivia Hillier, vintage clothing seller

The money Hillier makes from her gig helped her buy a house with a special "Poshmark" room that is given over to her inventory of over eleven hundred items. Hillier offers this advice to those who wish to launch a similar gig: "You've got to be regimented and have a routine. If I didn't love it so much, I wouldn't make the time for it."[30]

## Commit to the Gig

Hillier's gig is a success because she has the physical space to run her business. She has the financial resources to buy inventory and the tools she needs, including a washing machine, iron, a reliable car, and good lights and other studio equipment. Hillier also has good people skills: she can effectively communicate and interact with others. But Hillier says she still had to learn how to deal with unpleasant customers who complain and make unrea-

*Some gig jobs require good communication skills. You may have to deal with unpleasant customers who complain and make unreasonable demands.*

sonable demands. She admits, "It's hard to negotiate with people sometimes, and you can't please everyone."[31]

Hillier is able to run her business from her home, but other types of gigs might require you to ask yourself basic questions about personal safety. If you want to take on a gig as a driver or messenger, are you comfortable dealing with all sorts of people in many different types of situations? Do you feel safe working alone on the streets?

Plunging into the gig economy can be as challenging or enjoyable as you make it. With a small effort, you can earn extra spending money with a blog or other simple pursuit. If you have an eye for business and a willingness to commit time and energy to your gig, you can steer it toward a long-term career. Success does not always come easy, but if you are willing to make a plan, keep good records, learn from your mistakes, and commit time and energy to your gig, you just might be able pay your bills doing something you love—or at least something you want to do for a while.

## CHAPTER FOUR

# Making the Gig Economy Work for You

Some people work for the gig economy. They are laborers who provide services based on the terms dictated by their gig platforms. The apps push them to work certain times and decide how much they earn for each gig. Those who work for the gig economy are left to deal with tough schedules, gig-related expenses, nasty customers, and other problems. Working for the gig economy can feel like a thankless task with little to recommend it. As Yong Kim, chief executive officer of the employment website Wonolo, writes, "There are many gig work platforms that have created ecosystems where gig workers are not able to earn a living wage."[32]

Those who do not wish to deal with the downside of major gig platforms try to make the gig economy work for them. They create their own gig ecosystems using the tools that drive the gig economy, including social media, online marketing sites, video tutorials, and laptops and cell phones. Those who make the gig economy work for them have options. They can participate in the gig economy to earn a little extra money on the side or use it to turn a side hustle into a full-time career.

### Buying and Selling

High school student Max Hayden found a way to use the online retail site Amazon as a tool for success. In 2020, sixteen-year-old Hayden launched an e-commerce business in Hopewell, New Jersey. Hayden's gig is termed *reselling*: he purchases hard-to-find goods locally and resells them on Amazon at a higher price.

Hayden was always interested in buying and selling. In middle school, he earned pocket money by selling cheap fidget spinners he purchased in bulk to his friends. His first major success came during the 2020 COVID-19 lockdown when the pandemic forced all gyms to shut down. Hayden purchased dozens of 5 pound (2 kg) dumbbells at a local big box store. Within weeks the cost of dumbbells had tripled on Amazon, and Hayden resold his supply at a good profit. Hayden conducted research online to determine what other locally available items were selling at a higher cost on Amazon. This led him to make bulk purchases of other items that were suddenly in high demand during the lockdown. He bought dozens of PlayStations and Xbox machines for around $500 and resold them for $1,100. He did the same with webcams, backyard swimming pools, outdoor heaters, sewing machines, and bread makers.

While many shoppers were scrambling to buy products that were in short supply, Hayden had a secret. He paid around fifty dollars a month for membership in a platform called Discord. The platform notifies members when specific products are being restocked at Walmart, Target, and other big-box stores. This allowed Hayden to put in orders for high-demand items before others knew they were available.

Hayden set up a warehouse and distribution center in his parents' garage. By the end of 2020, he had made more than $110,000 in profits. Hayden says, "There are a lot of people in the reselling world that are high school age, college age, and it is really impressive that so many young people that are typically excluded from the business world are suddenly interested."[33]

> "There are a lot of people in the reselling world that are high school age. . . . It is really impressive that so many young people that are typically excluded from the business world are suddenly interested."[33]
>
> —Max Hayden, online reseller

*At the beginning of the COVID pandemic, resellers stocked up on home gym equipment at cheap prices. As gyms closed and people had to exercise at home, demand and prices for dumbbells and other equipment soared.*

Reselling large items can be grueling. Hayden often wrestles heavy boxes into the garage after they are delivered. While keeping a watchful eye on his Amazon resale site, MH Book Store, Hayden readies packages for shipping. He pays his two best friends fifteen dollars an hour to help him. UPS picks up the items every day and sends them out to buyers.

Hayden says the main drawback of his gig is that it takes so much of his time. In early 2021 he was dedicating forty hours a week to his resale business. After school restarted in September 2021, he had to shut down the business for a few months to get his grades back on track. And he has trouble maintaining a typical teenager's social life when he is constantly combing websites to find items to resell. But Hayden was looking forward to moving into a retail commercial space dedicated to his business. "If you have the drive and the goal of becoming a successful businessperson," he remarks, "you're going to be able to do it, even if you are a young person."[34]

Hayden is one of countless Gen Z consumers earning money online in nontraditional ways. They use Amazon as well as other resale apps, such as Goat and StockX. One of the most popular apps, Depop, is a combination of a social media site and a marketplace that is described as a cross between eBay and Instagram. Depop makes it easy to list and purchase items while engaging with a community of like-minded young shoppers. According to Depop vice president Rachel Swidenbank, 90 percent of its 13 million users worldwide are younger than twenty-six, and some Depop resellers make as much as $300,000 annually (the site takes a 10 percent cut on each transaction). Swidenbank says many Depop users are on the cutting edge of fashion trends, and the site has gained notice from the fashion industry: "A lot of people want to know what Gen Z is up to at the moment, what they are thinking, and what they are searching for so it is definitely something that a lot of brands would love to get their hands on."[35]

## Passive Income

While major companies scope out fashion trends on platforms such as Depop, the brands also hire freelancers, called *affiliate marketers*. These gig workers promote brands on their blogs and social media sites and receive a commission when they increase traffic to product websites. Some of the biggest tech companies in the world, including Amazon, eBay, and Google, use affiliate programs to drive profits. The most successful affiliate marketers are known by another term: *social media influencers*. These fashion bloggers, makeup artists, chefs, and other high-profile influencers are paid to hype products on Instagram, YouTube, Pinterest, and their other social media sites.

Shannon Smith is not an influencer celebrity, or even a microcelebrity, but she thought affiliate marketing might be a good fit for her. Smith turned to affiliate marketing after struggling to promote her own gig as a personal trainer. Smith had created a ninety-day fitness program that included personalized workouts, meal plans, and Zoom coaching sessions, but she found herself working ten-hour days yet averaging only $1,500 a month.

Although Smith did not make much money, she had built up a social media presence that would help her launch her new gig as an affiliate marketer. Smith knew little about how the gig worked, so she took an online course that showed her the best ways to get clicks while promoting products. In 2021 she used her TikTok and Instagram accounts to write blogs instructing others how to start side hustles and earn income online. These posts included mentions of her marketing affiliates along with links to their websites.

*Some gig workers, like personal trainers, can struggle on their own to make enough money and promote themselves. By working as an affiliate marketer too, they can supplement their income.*

## Plan for Slow Periods

Almost every gig worker knows what it is like to struggle financially because pay can be inconsistent. Or, as financial planner Roger Whitney states, "Your income may be irregular, but your bills aren't." Those who make the gig economy work for them prepare for slow periods by making smart moves when money is coming in. They pay off credit cards, put money into savings accounts, and invest in tools they need for their gigs. Financial experts recommend using a budgeting app to monitor expenses to gain a clear picture of how much you need to earn each month.

Alisha Eisenstock understands the difficulties posed by irregular income. To avoid running out of money, she works several gigs in unrelated fields, including tutoring, software development, and as a travel adviser for cruise ship customers. Eisenstock feels the gig economy is working for her, but money issues can be a hassle: "The money ebbs and flows. You have to always put some money aside because you don't know what's going to happen next. It's extremely unpredictable." Learning to budget and save is how successful gig workers keep their careers moving forward.

Quoted in Vox, "How to Make the Gig Economy Work for You," December 6, 2019. www.vox.com.

Within three months, Smith had forty-three thousand TikTok followers. Before long, she was earning over $8,000 a month in what is called *passive income*. This type of income is money that comes in with little or no effort on the part of the worker. Some of Smith's passive income comes from commissions from her affiliate posts, including those that are several months old but continue to pay. Her best passive income comes from recurring subscriptions that provide regular monthly commissions. In 2022 Smith wrote, "If you told me a year ago that I could do what I love—creating helpful content right from my phone and work just two hours a day—I would have laughed. I now have the freedom I'd always wanted. At 24 years old, I was able to move into a beautiful apartment in New York City, I get to travel frequently, and my life no longer revolves around work."[36]

"If you told me a year ago that I could do what I love—creaating helpful content right from my phone and work just two hours a day—I would have laughed."[36]

—Shannon Smith, affiliate marketer

Smith emphasizes that her success did not happen overnight. Her gig required her to initially spend money for expert guidance. Smith recommends that those who lack funds for an online course find a mentor in an online affiliate marketing community. She says she also invested a lot of time searching for good affiliate products to promote. Smith offers this advice:

> I recommend brainstorming a list of your hobbies and interests, then doing some research on the best affiliate programs in each category before narrowing your niche down to just one. . . . [For an] established account or website, your niche should match the content your audience already loves. If you have an Instagram account full of pictures with your dog, for example, look for affiliate products in the pet space.[37]

Smith also invested time honing her marketing skills. She searched online to learn how to write good advertising copy that would generate consumer interest. And her well-researched blogs provide a wealth of information that keeps subscribers coming back for more.

### Blogging for Brands

Gabby Beckford was a college student when she launched her travel blog *Packs Light* as a hobby. Beckford continued to write the blog after she started her career as a biomedical engineer at age twenty-three in 2018. Beckford felt that writing a blog was much more interesting than her engineering job. But she only brought in a few thousand dollars creating travel-related content focused on young women of color. Beckford dreamed of quitting to become a full-time world traveler but decided to move slowly and strategically toward her goal.

As an engineer, Beckford earned around $69,000 annually. She figured she needed to save around $15,000 before she could

*Blogging is a popular side gig but it can be difficult to make money doing it. Successful bloggers often partner with brands and companies to influence and help promote products and services. This can also lead to activities like free travel.*

take her blog gig to a more professional level. This led her into the side hustle economy. Beckford took jobs dog sitting, freelance writing, and managing social media accounts for others. She used the idle time while riding the subway to write travel articles, using a voice-to-text app. On her lunch breaks, she interviewed young travelers she wanted to feature in a special series on *Packs Light*.

Although it can be difficult to make money blogging, Beckford found the key to success. She marketed herself to travel agencies as a travel influencer. She inquired about what kind of influencer partnerships they were seeking. She then pitched them ideas based on their answers. For example, one travel website was looking for an influencer who had a young Black American audience interested in buying their travel tours and activities. Beckford conducted a survey among her followers that showed they were interested in traveling to Mexico. Based on that research, the travel company paid Beckford $3,000 to write blogs that promoted their Mexico travel campaign.

Beckford quit her engineering job in 2020, and within a year she had landed twelve brand partnership campaign contracts. The brands, which include North Face, Delta Airlines, and Adidas, each paid around $10,000. These marketers pay Beckford for sponsored posts, blogs, photos, and videos that feature their product. Beckford also earned passive income from blog ads, paid memberships, and sales of online courses for aspiring digital nomads.

### Passionate and Sincere

By 2022 Beckford had over 50,000 followers on Instagram and 250,000 on TikTok. She was earning around $20,000 a month. Beckford says the secret to her success is she had a clear vision of what she calls her "why," or the main reason she became a travel blogger:

> It's more important to establish your "why" early on. I have a deep and genuine love for traveling. I'm passionate about showing young women from all walks of life how they can find joy and meaning through travel—without all the planning stress that it typically comes with. Someone who knows their "why" is more authentic and attractive to clients and customers because it makes clear that they enjoy their work and are motivated by their mission.[38]

To carry out her mission, Beckford learned how to conduct research into the wants and needs of her audience and her clients. She also taught herself the necessary skills for creating an attractive website, including writing, photography, graphic design, and marketing. While doing so, she applied for business grants and participated in pitch competitions where contestants present their business ideas to a panel of experts in the hope of winning cash prizes. And once her gig started to grow, Beckford built a team to help her with her business. In 2022 she employed a blog manager, a personal assistant, and a group of marketing contractors who help drive traffic to her website. Although paying employees cuts into Beckford's profits, having others perform basic tasks allows her to spend more time pursuing money-making contracts.

> "It's more satisfying to be able to say 'I'm financially free' or 'I'm doing what I love every day' or 'I'm making an impact.'"[39]
>
> —Gabby Beckford, travel blogger

Despite being a successful entrepreneur, Beckford says she is not motivated by money. "It's more satisfying to be able to say 'I'm financially free' or 'I'm doing what I love every day' or 'I'm making an impact,'" she explains. "To be successful, you have to remember your 'why' and keep going. The financial success will eventually follow."[39]

Beckford's success is impressive, but like many social media influencers she is charismatic and photogenic. When she discusses a product she is paid to promote, her camera presence gives fans the feeling that she is a sincere best friend. Beckford's videos are high quality, on topic, and upbeat.

## Putting It All to Work

There are hundreds of success stories like Beckford's about people who make the gig economy work for them. And whatever the gig, the people behind those success stories use similar skills to gain and maintain their success. They create multiple social media accounts to market products on Twitter, Instagram, Facebook, Pinterest, Tumblr, Snapchat, and other platforms. Successful gig hustlers continually post photos, drawings, videos, memes, GIFs, and other marketing content. They use their communication skills to develop a unique "voice" and personality used to write engaging blogs and text messages meant to spark interest in topics related to their gig. And they become adept at customer relations; they correspond with people who have questions about a product and who comment on the posts.

If you want to make the gig economy work for you, remember that it requires constant effort. Most posts have a very short

## Setting Up an Online Resale Store

Many people have discovered that reselling products at a profit is the fastest way to get into the gig economy. And most major retail sites allow sellers to create custom storefronts to showcase their products. Depop is extremely popular with young fashionistas, and the site makes it easy to start selling. All you need to do is pick a catchy name for your shop. The site allows you to post a short bio to explain your fashion sense in a few words. Depop recommends posting four photos for each item: one lying flat, two close-ups, and one model shot. Write good, detailed descriptions of each item and be honest about the quality. Items with three hashtags sell the best, according to Depop. Once you set up shop, promote it on all your social media feeds. Follow the "Top Sellers" link on the Depop site to find out what the most successful people are selling and how they build their brands. After you complete a sale, encourage your customers to write reviews that can be shared. With these simple steps you can be buying and reselling clothes and accessories within a few hours.

life span. On Twitter, the average tweet is considered relevant for about fifteen minutes, and a Facebook post has a life of around six hours. Instagram posts are seen by the most people within the first twenty-four hours, whereas YouTube, Pinterest, and blogs have the longest life spans.

Posting content on a regular basis is important, but you should also be aware of when to post. For example, studies show that Facebook posts attract the most clicks on Saturday and Sunday afternoon, whereas tweeting is most effective around 5 p.m. on weekdays. Instagram is busiest on Monday and Thursday nights, and one of the best times to post videos is 2 a.m. You also need to consider time zones when posting—2 a.m. in Los Angeles is 5 a.m. in New York. But it is not necessary to stay up all night to do the job properly. Scheduling tools such as Hootsuite, Buffer, and TweetDeck allow users to bulk schedule multiple posts.

Successful online gig workers need to know if the content they create is reaching its intended audience. This requires them to keep track of analytics—information from websites and mobile apps about page and post likes, engagement rate (likes, shares, comments), and user demographics. Most people with online businesses use analytic tools, including Google Analytics, Iconosquare (Instagram), and Meta Business Suite (Facebook). This might sound very complicated, but social media analyst Alice Fuller explains that you can "learn the fundamentals of marketing and writing first. Learn as much as you can . . . then put what you learn into practice for yourself, [or] work with others for free or [a] low fee so you can get some real experience under your belt."[40]

One of the most positive aspects of the gig economy is that it is only as limited as your talent, curiosity, and willingness to work. With billions of people online every day searching for goods, services, and advice, there is unlimited potential for those who want to make the gig economy work for them. Focus on what you want, research what people need, and shape your future using the tools at your fingertips.

> "Learn the fundamentals of marketing and writing first. Learn as much as you can . . . then put what you learn into practice for yourself."[40]
>
> —Alice Fuller, social media analyst

# SOURCE NOTES

### Introduction: Not a Traditional Job

1. Quoted in Michael B. Horn, "What the 'Gig' Economy Means for Graduates and Their Employers," *Forbes*, October 20, 2016. www.forbes.com.
2. Diane Mulcahy, *The Gig Economy*. New York: American Management Association, 2016, p. 30.
3. Deanna Ritchie, "10 Golden Rules to Making Money Online Without Risking Everything," *Entrepreneur*, May 14, 2022. www.entrepreneur.com.

### Chapter One: What Is the Gig Economy?

4. Nikhil Bansal, "Uberization of the Economy," Medium, June 4, 2019. https://medium.com.
5. Mulcahy, *The Gig Economy*, p. 28.
6. Quoted in Perri Ormont Blumberg, "I'm a 23-Year-Old Who's Made More than $130,000 on TaskRabbit This Year—Here's How," Insider, November 15, 2021. www.businessinsider.com.
7. Quoted in Dani Anguiano, "'It's Not Worth It': Rising Gas Prices Force Drivers to Work for Less than Minimum Wage," *The Guardian*, March 10, 2022. www.theguardian.com.
8. Mulcahy, *The Gig Economy*, p. 30.
9. Quoted in Jackie Davalos and Drake Bennett, "Gamification Took Over the Gig Economy. Who's Really Winning?," Bloomberg, May 27, 2022. www.bloomberg.com.
10. Quoted in Davalos and Bennett, "Gamification Took Over the Gig Economy."
11. Davalos and Bennett, "Gamification Took Over the Gig Economy."
12. Kartik Menon, "Investors, Customers, and Workers Are Fed Up with Delivery Apps," Insider, May 25, 2022. www.businessinsider.com.

### Chapter Two: Are Gig Jobs Right for You?

13. Kyle Nossaman, "A Year in a Skoolie: What We Love (and What We Don't)," *Gear Junkie*, January 19, 2019. https://gearjunkie.com.
14. Quoted in Ariel Felton, "When #Vanlife Meets the $300 Tank," *New York Times*, June 15, 2022. www.nytimes.com.

15. Quoted in Elaine Pofeldt, "The Gig Economy Happiness Gap," *Forbes*, February 13, 2016. www.forbes.com.
16. Sut I. Wong, "Job Crafting Can Help Digital Workers Build Resilience," *Harvard Business Review*, January 12, 2022. https://hbr.org.
17. Wong, "Job Crafting Can Help Digital Workers Build Resilience."
18. Thomas Oppong, "This Is How to Increase the Odds of Reaching Your Goals by 95%," Pocket Worthy, 2022. https://getpocket.com.
19. Allison Nichol Longtin, "I Turned My Creative Passion into a Lucrative Side Hustle That Earns Me Up to 40% of My Income as a Freelancer," *Personal Finance* (blog), Insider, April 20, 2022. www.businessinsider.com.
20. Longtin, "I Turned My Creative Passion into a Lucrative Side Hustle That Earns Me Up to 40% of My Income as a Freelancer."
21. Longtin, "I Turned My Creative Passion into a Lucrative Side Hustle That Earns Me Up to 40% of My Income as a Freelancer."
22. Quoted in Carolyn Ockels, Steve King, and Gene Zaino, "Workers Don't Feel Like a 9-to-5 Job Is a Safe Bet Anymore," *Harvard Business Review*, March 23, 2022. https://hbr.org.
23. Quoted in Pofeldt, "The Gig Economy Happiness Gap."
24. Quoted in Mitchell Harman, "What Makes Gig Economy Workers Anxious?," Marketplace, March 8, 2018. www.marketplace.org.

## Chapter Three: Plunging In

25. Vicky Chen, "Intention," *Vicky Again* (blog), January 10, 2020. https://vickyagain.wordpress.com.
26. Quoted in Goh Chiew Tong, "From Baker to Entrepreneur, How This High-School Grad Built Up His $100,000 Business," CNBC, May 17, 2022. www.cnbc.com.
27. Quoted in Chiew Tong, "From Baker to Entrepreneur, How This High-School Grad Built Up His $100,000 Business."
28. Brett Helling, "Entrepreneurship 101: Business Plan Examples," Gigworker, August 1, 2019. https://gigworker.com.
29. Quoted in Megan Sauer, "This 26-Year-Old Med Student Bought a House by Selling Used Clothes: Without the Side Hustle, 'I Wouldn't Even Have a Savings Account,'" CNBC, May 11, 2022. www.cnbc.com.
30. Quoted in Sauer, "This 26-Year-Old Med Student Bought a House by Selling Used Clothes."
31. Quoted in Sauer, "This 26-Year-Old Med Student Bought a House by Selling Used Clothes."

## Chapter Four: Making the Gig Economy Work for You

32. Yong Kim, "Are Gig Economy Workers Being Exploited?," *Forbes*, November 20, 2019. www.forbes.com.
33. Quoted in Sunny Kim, "This 16-Year-Old's Company Brings In Millions Buying from Walmart and Selling on Amazon," CNBC, July 28, 2021. www.cnbc.com.
34. Quoted in Kim, "This 16-Year-Old's Company Brings In Millions Buying from Walmart and Selling on Amazon."
35. Quoted in Mary Hanbury, "Teens Are Getting Rich Off This Social Shopping App as Their Shopping Habits Change the Fashion Industry," Insider, April 28, 2019. www.businessinsider.com.
36. Shannon Smith, "This 24-Year-Old Lost Her Waitressing Job. Now She Makes $8,600 per Month in Passive Income: 'I Work Just 2 hours a Day,'" CNBC, January 19, 2022. www.cnbc.com.
37. Smith, "This 24-Year-Old Lost Her Waitressing Job."
38. Gabby Beckford, "This 26-Year-Old Quit Her Engineering Job to Pursue Her Side Hustle Full-Time—and Brought in $170,000 in One Year," CNBC, January 10, 2022. www.cnbc.com.
39. Gabby Beckford, "This 26-Year-Old Turned Her Side Hustle into a $170,000-per-Year Business: '4 Things I Wish I Knew Sooner,'" CNBC, March 17, 2022. www.cnbc.com.
40. Quoted in David Finch, "How to Get a Social Media Manager Job," Social Media Explorer, September 11, 2020. https://socialmediaexplorer.com.

# FOR FURTHER RESEARCH

## Books

Heidi Ayarbe, *Gig Jobs in High-Tech*. San Diego: BrightPoint, 2022.

Will Eagle, *Making TikTok Videos*. Needham, MA: For Dummies, 2023.

Bridey Heing, ed., *The Gig Economy*. New York: Greenhaven, 2020.

Stuart A. Kallen, *Teen Guide to Side Gigs: Working in the New Economy*. San Diego: ReferencePoint, 2022.

Clara MacCarald, *Gig Jobs in the Creative Arts*. San Diego: BrightPoint, 2022.

## Internet Articles

Nikhil Bansal, "Uberization of the Economy," Medium, June 4, 2019. https://medium.com.

Perri Ormont Blumberg, "I'm a 23-Year-Old Who's Made More than $130,000 on TaskRabbit This Year—Here's How," Insider, November 15, 2021. www.businessinsider.com.

Jackie Davalos and Drake Bennett, "Gamification Took Over the Gig Economy. Who's Really Winning?," Bloomberg, May 27, 2022. www.bloomberg.com.

Mary Hanbury, "Teens Are Getting Rich Off This Social Shopping App as Their Shopping Habits Change the Fashion Industry," Insider, April 28, 2019. www.businessinsider.com.

Brett Helling, "Entrepreneurship 101: Business Plan Examples," Gigworker, August 1, 2019. https://gigworker.com.

Sut I. Wong, "Job Crafting Can Help Digital Workers Build Resilience," *Harvard Business Review*, January 12, 2022. https://hbr.org.

## Websites

### Financial Wolves
https://financialwolves.com
This website features ideas for side hustles, delivery app reviews, online moneymaking strategies, and other information about the gig economy. It offers advice and charts trends relevant to young entrepreneurs.

### Gig Economy Tax Center

www.irs.gov/businesses/gig-economy-tax-center

The IRS provides this website for self-employed workers who need help figuring out their taxes. Visitors to the site can download tax forms, watch an explanatory video, and learn about deductions and self-employment taxes.

### Gig Workers Collective

www.gigworkerscollective.org

This nonprofit group is fighting for better pay and treatment for gig economy workers with a focus on grocery shoppers and rideshare drivers. Visitors can learn about the various causes and donate their support.

### Mobile Workers Alliance (MWA)

https://mobilealliance.org

The MWA is made up of drivers who use apps such as Uber, Lyft, DoorDash, and Postmates to earn their paychecks. The organization is fighting for better pay and working conditions for rideshare and delivery drivers.

### Starter Story

www.starterstory.com

Starter Story interviews people who have turned their side hustles into successful businesses. Entrepreneurs are asked how they got started, how they grew their businesses, and what it takes to compete.

# INDEX

*Note: Boldface page numbers indicate illustrations.*

affiliate marketers, 45–48
Aria, David, 28–**29**
artificial intelligence, in management of gig workers, 14–17
Association for Talent Development, 25–26

Bansal, Nikhil, 10
Beckford, Gabby, 48–51
Bennett, Drake, 17
blogging, 31–33
bookstagrammers, 33
business essentials, learning, 7
business plans, 38–40

Campbell, Harry, 17
casual earners, **12**–13
Chase, Robin, 4–5
Chen, Vicky, 33
COVID-19 pandemic, 13, 15, 39, 43

Davalos, Jackie, 17
Depop (resale app), 45, 52
Discord (web platform), 43

DoorDash (food delivery app), 18

Eisenstock, Alisha, 47
Ellen, Justin, 35–36, 37
Estrada, Jupiter, 22

Facebook (social media platform), 51, 52
Financial Wolves (website), 57
Fiorita, Tom, 11
Fiverr (freelance employment platform), 10
forty/forty plan, 20
freelancers
  number of people identified as, 10
  subgroups of, 11–13

Gantt, Rondu, 13–14
gig economy
  blogging and, 31–**32**
  definition of, 8
  economics of, 17
  lack of profits in platforms of, 17–19
  winners and losers in, 13–14
Gig Economy Tax Center (website), 58
GigPoint (benefits app), 11

Gig Workers Collective, 25, 58
Goat (resale app), 45
Grabr (app), 10
Grubhub (food delivery app), 10

Hayden, Max, 42–45
Helling, Brett, 38
Hillier, Olivia, 39–**41**

income taxes, 36–38, 39
Instacart (gig platform), 10, 31
Instagram, 33
Instagram (social media platform), 51, 52
Internal Revenue Service (IRS), 36, 39

job insecurity, dealing with, 22–25

Kim, Yong, 42
King, Steve, 22, 28
Kunert, Torsten, 17

Longtin, Allison Nichol, 26–28, **29**

MBO Partners, 28
McKinsey Global Institute, 10
Menon, Kartik, 18
Mobile Workers Alliance (MWA), 58
Mulcahy, Diane, 5, 11, 14

Newland, Stephen, 27
Nossaman, Kyle, **21**–22

opinion polls. *See* surveys
Oppong, Thomas, 26
opportunity mindset, 5

Pew Research Center, 15, 17
Pinterest (social media platform), 51
polls. *See* surveys
Poshmark (website), 39, 40
posting, on social media platforms, 51–53

Randstad (employment website), **21**
record keeping, 36–38
reluctant workers, 13
research, 5–7
reselling, 43–45, 52
*Rideshare Guy* (blog), 17
rideshares, **6**, 17
   use of artificial intelligence by, 15–17
Ritchie, Deanna, **6**

self-promotion, **6**, 31, 33
   creating website for, 34–35
   using social media, **46**–48
shipping and handling, 37
Smith, Shannon, 45–48
Snapchat (social media platform), 51
social media influencers, 45

Starter Story (website), 58
stickK (accountability app), 27
StockX (resale app), 45
surveys
  on attitudes toward traditional employment, **21**
  on feelings about gig work, 15
  on feeling secure in independent work, 28
  on gig workers' understanding of pay calculation, 17
Swidenbank, Rachel, 45

TaskRabbit (gig platform), 10, 13, 31
Tumblr (social media platform), 51

Twitter (social media platform), 51, 52

Uber (ridesharing app), 9
  experience of driver for, 13–14
Upwork (freelance employment platform), 10

*Vicky Who Reads* (blog), 33

websites, creating, **34**–35
Whitney, Roger, 47
Wong, Sut I., 22–23, 25
WordPress (blogging website), 33, **34**

Young, William, 13, 14

# PICTURE CREDITS

Cover: Lia Koltyrina/Shutterstock.com

6: Snap-PhotoProduction/Shutterstock.com
9: Andrey Armyagor/Shutterstock.com
12: Gorodenkoff/Shutterstock.com
16: amirraizat/Shutterstock.com
21: Jacob Lund/Shutterstock.com
24: Lordn/Shutterstock.com
29: Ground Picture/Shutterstock.com
32: hedgehog94/Shutterstock.com
34: David MG/Shutterstock.com
41: fizkes/Shutterstock.com
44: Megan Czarhocki/Shutterstock.com
46: fizkes/Shutterstock.com
49: Dragon Images/Shutterstock.com

## ABOUT THE AUTHOR

Stuart A. Kallen is the author of more than 350 nonfiction books for children and young adults. He has written on topics ranging from the theory of relativity to the art of electronic dance music. In 2018 Kallen won a Green Earth Book Award from the Nature Generation environmental organization for his book *Trashing the Planet: Examining the Global Garbage Glut*. In his spare time, he is a singer, songwriter, and guitarist in San Diego.